9-08

RENOIR

By: ALBERTO MARTINI

AVENEL BOOKS

NEW YORK

Renoir © MCMLXXVIII by Fabbri Editori, Milan, Italy
English Translation Copyright © by Fabbri Editori, Milan, Italy
All Rights Reserved
First U.S. Edition published 1978 by Avenel Books
distributed by Crown Publishers Inc.
Printed in Italy by Fabbri Editori, Milan.
a   b   c   d   e   f   g   h   i

Library of Congress Cataloging in Publication Data
Renoir, Auguste, 1841-1919.
Renoir.
1. Renoir, Auguste, 1841-1919. I. Martini, Alberto. II. Title.
ND553.R45A4 1978 759.4 78-18883
ISBN 0-517-24955-3

Renoir's life can be divided into two periods. In his youth, he worked as a craftsman and dreamed of becoming a painter. Later, when he had become a great artist, his dreams came true every time he worked on a canvas. Renoir always considered painting as a craft, and apart from his dream-inspired artistic experiences and his masterpieces, his life was uneventful.

Pierre-Auguste Renoir was born in Limoges on February 25, 1841. He came from a family of workmen. Renoir's father, a modest tailor hoping to improve his precarious financial situation, moved to Paris when his son was four. At the age of fourteen, already expressing an interest in art, Renoir was sent to work with a porcelain painter. In the evenings he attended free drawing classes. In 1858 Renoir abandoned porcelain painting and began painting fabrics and fans in order to earn more money. Young Renoir showed great manual ability and surprising speed in the execution of his work.

Having saved some money, in 1862 he entered the Beaux-Arts studio of Gleyre. There he met other young painters—Monet, Bazille, Sisley—with whom he would remain friends for the rest of his life. The following year he regularly went to the Louvre to copy ancient art, as well as to Chailly in the forest of Fontainebleau, where he met an old master of the Barbizon School, Narcisso Diaz, who taught him to appreciate nature, color and light. Renoir lived through these years with enthusiasm, even though he often found himself in financial difficulties. Occasionally some of his paintings were accepted at the Salon, the large government-sponsored art exhibition which was held every year in Paris. But most of the time his works were refused, for they were too closely connected with the modern art movement. Renoir idolized Courbet, who was considered a revolutionary and a corrupter of good painting. Yet it was all but impossible to sell any paintings without being accepted at the Salon. Fortunately, Bazille, who came from a wealthy family, accepted Renoir in his studio and helped him financially.

In 1868, Renoir's painting Lise was accepted at the Salon and brought him some recognition. By now introduced to the Parisian artistic circles, Renoir often met with the group that included Manet (who assumed the role of a master), Degas, Bazille, Sisley, Monet, Pissarro, Cezanne, Fantin-Latour, the photographer Nadar, and the critics and writers Astruc, Duranty, Duret and Zola. It was during these meetings that the idea of a group show arose—an exhibition of the Impressionists. But the realization of this project was postponed first by the Franco-Prussian war of 1870, then by disagreements among the artists and by financial problems. The exhibition opened finally in 1874, thanks in large measure to Renoir's enthusiasm.

The exhibition, which was set up in Nadar's photographic studio, caused an enormous scandal. People laughed or felt shocked and angry. The show was a success although it presented the work of painters who had been so often turned down or poorly exhibited at the official Salons. One of the results of this exhibition, organized again in 1876, 1877, 1879 and 1882, was that it increased the number of people who appreciated the Impressionists. A second result was that the Impressionists gained more and more confidence in themselves. This was also due in part to the support they received from the enlightened art dealer Durand-Ruel.

During these years, Renoir was close to Monet. They often painted together, walking along the Seine, visiting the Paris suburbs. Renoir eventually traveled around the country, meeting friends and acquaintances, painting their portraits, and looking for locations which were congenial to his artistic sensibility. In 1880 he fell in love with one of his models, Aline Charigot, who became his wife. A year later, in 1881, he made a trip to Italy. His discovery of Raphael's paintings and Pompeian wall frescoes were to have a great influence on his stylistic development. By this time Renoir had become quite well known and reasonably well off. The time had not yet arrived, however, for a complete acceptance of the Impressionists. Renoir went through a complicated struggle with the French Government about the art collection that Caillebote left to the state.

Caillebote was a friend of Renoir's and had appointed the painter executor of his will. It took three years for the government to accept this most important collection, which it did only after it had reduced the number of paintings it took, especially those by Cezanne.

During this period, Renoir began to have his first attacks of rheumatism. He moved to the South of France and spent the winter of 1899 in Cagnes, where he settled permanently in 1905. In 1912 his illness worsened, forcing him to paint with brushes strapped to his hand. But even in this condition, his enthusiasm as well as his creativity did not diminish. He died in Cagnes, on the third of December 1919, after having paid his last visit to the Louvre where his paintings now hung next to those of other masters he had loved all his life.

3

"A new image of the world through a successful harmony of visual emotions and impressions."

The Bathers—Paris, The Louvre.

"No doubt you paint to amuse yourself, don't you?" With this disapproving question, the academician Gleyre addressed the young Renoir who had just entered his atelier at the Ecole des Beaux Arts. "Of course," replied the student, "and please do believe that if it didn't amuse me I wouldn't even paint."

This short anecdote allows us to understand the nature of the relationship that tied Renoir to painting. To him, painting was pleasure in the highest sense of the word, a joyful act which was repeated each time the colors began to create lyrical images on the canvas. It was a pleasure and an exaltation of the senses. If Renoir had to choose between representing a flower or an "idea," he would not hesitate, he would choose the flower. It was not that he looked down on the intellectual values which always come into play in a work of art; but because of his temperament Renoir was attracted to what was alive, to what viewers could relate to. Even the most common and humble of flowers expressed the life and nourishment of nature, which allowed everything to germinate and grow. Flowers contain the simple and eternal beauty of the world. Renoir wanted to experience everything as if it belonged to an indestructible unity of air and light. It was his way of participating in the great flow of life. In a picture of a flower, one can instinctively understand these pantheistic concepts, but in the abstract representation of an idea the true essence of a flower cannot be expressed. To Renoir, as well as to all the other Impressionists, the respect of reality was an absolutely fundamental principle. Reality now expressed a unified emotional content where images are filtered through a lyrical relation between the eye and one's emotions, from observation to transfiguration. It was a balance which Monet, Pissarro and Sisley, who were the closest to Renoir among the Impressionists, each defined in his own particular manner. What set Renoir apart and was characteristic of his approach was his warm, personal closeness to his subjects and his use of sumptuous colors. People or objects were transformed as they were painted in beautiful and lively scenes. Renoir used lighter and more luminous tones to express the delicate and exquisite grace of his tender and lyrical emotions. His vision cheerfully shifted between earth and sky, jumped from one cloud to another, as from

The Dreamer—Saint Louis, The City Art Museum.

face to face. The world was a festival of colors and light. How could he translate the shifting emotions stimulated by these experiences? How could he not paint these wonderful visions? Only painting could be this marvelous instrument of communication. Painting allows us to display our emotions and our sensitivity and to communicate these feelings to others. Through the medium of his work, Renoir's humanity, his exaltation and enthusiasm for life, have become our heritage.

Renoir was a naturalist, in the fullest sense of the word. He needed to feel the physical presence of figures or landscape when he painted. He wanted to provoke a direct confrontation with reality. But for Renoir it was not a violent gesture, an attempt to possess reality as it was for Courbet, but rather a gentle caress, both lyrical and sensual, which emanated from his immense love of life. "I like paintings that make me want to walk into them if they are landscapes, to caress them if they depict women." This sentence typifies Renoir's artistic vision.

While his paintings appeared to be effortless and spontaneous, they were the result of long periods of experimentation and suffering. In 1862, after the night classes which he attended while he was still working as a decorator, he enrolled in the Beaux Arts studio of Gleyre. At the Ecole he experimented with traditional art styles. Encouraged by his friend Fantin-Latour, he spent long hours copying the works of old masters in the Louvre.

In Gleyre's atelier Renoir met and became friends with other young students such as Monet, Sisley and Bazille, who were to become future participants in the Impressionist movement. At the time, however, they had not yet thought of changing the representation of reality and only wanted to achieve a mastery of painting techniques. But, unlike other fellow students, they considered these techniques a means, not an end. They also preferred painting outdoors, in the open and from real life, instead of following the formal studio academic exercises that evoked scenes from legends or mythology. Unlike other students, they were interested in the most advanced researches of contemporary art. For these reasons, besides attending classes at the academy or visiting the Louvre, they went to the forest of Fontainebleau, the real training school of modern naturalism. Renoir's meeting with the old painter Diaz

Dance in the Country—Private collection.

was critical in that this accomplished master of the Barbizon school taught him how to liberate himself from somber tones, and to observe and paint the wonders of nature in all their glorious color and light.

The young painter continued to experiment. In his paintings, Renoir alternated between the traditional drawing methods outlining the composition, the use of a wider range of pigments in Courbet's style (his new idol), and a pure, pre-impressionistic visual and atmospheric style. It was not a dramatic dilemma for Renoir because he was aware that he had not yet found himself as a painter or discovered his poetical world. But he was excited with the prospect of proving to himself his capacity to imitate the paintings of the artists he admired. Painting was the impossible goal of the poor boy who decorated china and who cried when someone teasingly called him "Rubens." But his dream had now become reality, and he was intoxicated with joy, trying all the methods which were now open to him, experimenting with all the styles of painting. He wanted to explore the whole of the art world, so he could claim it as his own.

His only guide was his sensibility. His only scope, for the present as well as for the future, was pleasure.

In his mature years he often changed his stylistic language, but the subdivision into different periods that some critics use are exaggerated. They do not take into account the unity of his attitude toward life and nature. For this reason, we will not dwell on abstract and formal distinctions. It is more important to explain the stylistic progression that animated the entire course of his work. It was the method of an artist who had the courage to be himself. He had the courage to question his own work; he remained open to the experiences which he felt were congenial to his personality; and he rejected all theoretical considerations. Renoir's focus was on color and form, on the visual and atmospheric rendering of reality and its tactile and plastic expression. Even though he sometimes stressed one particular idea, his paintings never expressed an absolute and exclusive choice. He tried to use more than one idea in order to come as close as possible to the reality of his observation, to the reality of the visual and emotional atmosphere which surrounded his subjects. Only when he had

7

created a balance between nature and reality as expressed through the different aspects of his sensibility, did he consider his painting finished.

Between 1864 and 1867, during a passionate search for his own style, he experienced his greatest artistic growth. Renoir took an active part in art discussions of the period, and after having supported Diaz and the vigorous Courbet, he sided with Manet, with whom he always shared a love of contemporary life. In the *Inn of Mere Anthony* (Stockholm, National Museum), painted in Marlotte in 1866, one can feel the sense of close identification with the contemporary world he liked so much. The painting also reveals Renoir's rejection of Courbet's tonality in order to combine the weightlessness and vibrations of light with the lyrical quality of his own colors. It was a first timid step, which seemed to have been forgotten the following year in his *Huntress Diana* (Washington, National Gallery of Art), where Courbet's influence once more dominated.

In the course of that year, however, Renoir returned to the contemporary world with his beautiful painting *Lise* (Essen, Volkwang Museum). It was painted outdoors, in the forest of Fontainebleau. It is the work of a mature painter and the affirmation of a new and original artistic personality. It did not have the frankness of Manet's chromatic imprint, or the detailed optical analysis which characterises Monet's paintings. It presents the harmonious luminosity of Renoir's soft colors and an aura that permeates and penetrates the substance of form. No one had yet so clearly seen the relationship between a figure and its surroundings. "The effect is so natural and so real that one forces oneself to find it false, for we have been accustomed to see nature represented in conventional colors." This was the critic Burger's perceptive comment in a review of the Salon of 1868, where Renoir's painting was exhibited. What was astonishing was Renoir's acute observation of the shadows, colored by the reflections from the trees. It was something absolutely new and it seemed at first to be the result of Renoir's arbitrary freedom. But it was a genuine attempt to come closer to the appearance of reality, liberating the image from the conventional use of chiaroscuro and of neutral tones which gave paintings a cold harmony of colors. Along with Monet,

Pheasant on the Snow—Geneva, L.C. Stein.

whose *Dejeuner sur l'Herbe* was painted two years before *Lise*, Renoir found an important new direction for European painting, which expressed a new way of seeing and representing nature. Both Renoir and Monet have contributed to our understanding of reality, as is the case for any original artistic experience.

Relieved by the critics' words, and by Manet's interest in his painting, as well as by those of all his friends of the Cafe Guerbois—a meeting place on the Rue des Batignolles—Renoir felt that he had finally found an artistic direction and a stylistic dimension suited to his personality. In 1868 he painted *Sisley and his Wife in a Garden* (Cologne, WallRaff-Richartz Museum) and *Skaters in the Bois de Boulogne* (Basel Von Hirsch coll.). In these paintings his rapid brushstrokes and agitated rendering of scenes full of movement and life helped overcome Courbet's bulkiness.

Renoir stands alone among the painters of the group of the Batignolles, the Impressionists. They were not a school with an established program, however, but a community of artists who were eager to revive a declining tradition. Renoir demonstrated his sense of freedom and humanity and his enthusiasm for participating in the life of the period.

After *La Grenouillere* (Stockholm, National Museum) of 1869 and the views of the Pont Neuf, of the Seine, of the quays and boulevards, and of Argenteuil painted in the year of the first group show of Impressionists, he completed a number of masterpieces of grace, gentleness and penetrating observation such as *La Loge* (London, Courtauld Institute) and *Dancer* (Washington, National Gallery of Art). The theme of these paintings is still the relationship between a figure and its surroundings, but Renoir confronted and resolved the problem in a much bolder manner here than in the painting *Lise*. The forms are vaporous and graceful. They emerge from the pulsations of a light in a golden atmosphere and they are immersed in that airy substance that surrounds and dissolves them. The fantasy world of the great masters of the Rococo style, from Watteau to Boucher and Fragonard, belonged to Renoir's daily life and allowed him to reject mythological themes. He found that world in a young girl on a swing, in a woman reclining on a couch while reading a newspaper, in the festive dance at the Moulin de la Galette, in the intimate family reunions, in the innocent, naked bathers. The decade of the 1870s was certainly the happiest of his life. Renoir felt completely fulfilled and was creating images of the world as if he were in an enchanted greenhouse. Contemporary life, in all its different aspects, was his principal theme. He left us such serene and lyrical images of his time that we may regret not having lived through these years, even though we know that the paradise of his heart and vision was quite different from the reality of the world of his contemporaries.

In the years that followed, Renoir underwent a crisis that erupted in 1884, but it did not disturb the serenity of his spirit. It had its effects on his expressive language—his style. Renoir was disappointed and unhappy with his Impressionist paintings, with the freedom of its method of expression, and with the predominating visual analysis of the painters of his group. After having admired the Pompeian wall frescoes and Raphael, particularly at the

Renoir's Family—Merion (Penn.), The Barnes Foundation.

9

Farnesina, and having meditated over the works of Ingres, Delacroix's antagonist whom he continued to adore, Renoir felt that he still had a great deal to learn—particularly in drawing. During this period his paintings were characterized by a sudden firmness in their outlines, by a more rigorous plastic definition, which did not, however, exclude the Impressionistic touch. Renoir was too uninterested in a system of esthetic rules. He remained a completely instinctive artist who could not understand the critics disapproving his sudden change in style. He was only mastering his profession and improving his technique. His fantasy world remained the same, and the same human warmth animated the scenes that he painted—bathers or portraits, landscapes or still-lifes. Renoir was aware of the limitations of a purely visual relationship with the world. It could lead to a rigid schematization, or even to an almost scientific system, like the one Seurat had developed in those years. Unable to tolerate rules, he tried to detach himself and explored other directions, other possibilities. But he felt that these rigorously precise drawings exclude a sense of life and warmth, and that the colors were restricted within the formal structure of the work. At that point, he had no hesitation in abandoning them. He would no longer use the wide range of color of his early works. He discovered that the same color, spread out in vibrant and thick brushstrokes, could reconstruct the form and draw the image. Toward the end of his life, when Renoir moved closer to the warm sun of southern France, the entire universe began to emerge and to vibrate in the single immense, pantheistic emotion of his last paintings. The figures and their surroundings now related to each other with the same vital force, and the artist lived within them in the same pantheistic approach.

In Cagnes, his attacks of rheumatism and the paralysis of his lower limbs wracked his poor body. The old painter, eternally enamored of beauty and obsessed by his feeling for nature and man, proudly reacted to the approach of death. His passionate, vital exaltation transformed the brushes strapped to his paralyzed fingers into caressing feathers that were both lyrical and sensual. Color, light and life triumphed once again in a spacious and open song, vigorous and powerful, that could be compared only to the last works of Titian or to the best works of Rubens.

Jean Renoir dressed as Pierrot—Paris, Private collection.

VI - The Clown - Otterlo, Rijksmuseum Kröller-Müller - *The circus world had always fascinated those artists of the second half of the 19th century in France who had opposed the use of the traditional themes in academic painting, history, or classical and literary representations. Renoir, in this painting of 1868, has depicted the world of the circus which was so attractive to the young impressionists.*

VII - The Champs-Elysées during the Universal Exposition of 1867 - Zurich, private collection - *With this canvas Renoir resolutely adopted the new conceptions of the impressionists. He depicts a moment of life, the joyous animation of a place, the movement of the crowd, all inundated in that luminosity that was characteristic of the "plein-air" school of painting.*

VIII - The Pont des Arts and the Institut - Los Angeles, Norton Simon Foundation - *In this painting of 1868, in which one can detect the effect of the vibrating light that is particular to Renoir's paintings, the brushstrokes are still very clear, almost schematic. He has not yet elaborated that separation of colors that was to affirm itself during those years among the young Parisian painters.*

Index of the illustrations

I - Flowers in a Vase and a Champagne Glass - Private collection - *When Renoir painted this work in about 1866, the impressionist technique was not yet fully developed. The vigorous brushstrokes, the impasto of the thick colors remind one of Courbet, but a certain luminosity and a somewhat free interpretation already indicate his independent personality.*

IX - Claude Monet Reading - Paris, Musée Marmottan - *From 1862 Renoir was a close friend of Monet's. They often worked side-by-side at the forest of Fontainebleau or on the banks of the Seine, searching for a new vision of nature and its relationship to man. This portrait is of 1872, when Renoir was Monet's guest at Argenteuil.*

II - The Inn of Mère Anthony - Stockholm, Nationalmuseum - *Painted at Marlotte in 1866, this work demonstrates how Renoir was seeking his own individual style. Courbet's influence is still evident, but Renoir uses a lighter touch applied with a greater sense of freedom. His friend Sisley is on the right, the painter Le Coeur in the center, and standing, Monet.*

X - Summertime, or La Bohémienne - Berlin, Nationalgalerie - *In some of the portraits of Lise, the girl he had met in the house of his friend Jules Le Coeur, his favorite model, Renoir still used rather somber colors, but in this painting of 1868, he used a newer technique: the tones are lighter and the subject stands out from a contrasting background.*

III - Portrait of Renoir's Mother - Zurich, private collection - *In order to make a living Renoir was forced to work as a craftsman, which was not very satisfying for him. But he never abandoned his love for painting, and his continued search for a personal style of expression can be seen in his youthful works, such as in this portrait of 1860, when he was only 19 years old.*

XI - La Grenouillère - Stockholm, Nationalmuseum - *One can already clearly see the impressionistic innovations in this canvas of 1869. Renoir wanted to represent, with short and rapid brushstrokes and with the impression of immediacy, the reflection of the figures and objects in the water, the vibration of the light, the impression of a particular moment of serenity and harmony.*

IV - The Sisleys - Cologne, Wallraf-Richartz Museum - *When Renoir painted this work in 1868, he had already chosen to paint only contemporary scenes, abandoning the hesitations that in the preceding years had led him to depict traditional themes using a very academic style.*

XII - Woman with a Parrot - New York, Solomon R. Guggenheim Foundation, the Thannhauser Collection - *This is Renoir's last portrait of Lise Tréhot, a short time before the marriage of his model and friend. It is also one of the first works painted by the artist on his return to Paris from the Franco-Prussian War.*

V - Lise, the Woman with a Parasol - Essen, Folkwang Museum - *The life-size figure of Lise standing in front of a forest wearing a white dress that the green of the trees tinges with its reflections results from the careful observation of reality by which Renoir discovers the colors within the shadows that intensify the luminosity of the color. This first large portrait dates from 1867.*

XIII - Odalisque, or an Algerian Woman - Washington, National Gallery of Art, the Chester Dale Collection - *Painted in 1870, a short time before he enlisted to fight in the war of 1870 against the Germans, this portrait of Lise, shows the influence of Delacroix (whom Renoir greatly admired), not only in the composition, but in the use of colors as well.*

XIV - The Seine at Argenteuil - Portland, Ore., The Portland Art Museum Collection - *This painting, as the one of the Grenouillère, was painted by Renoir when in the company of Monet. Argenteuil was the village favored by the impressionist artists, who continued to paint there during those innovating years 1873-74.*

XV - Young Girl with a Dog - Paris, private collection - *Even when Renoir completely adapted the impressionist style, he always dealt with the human figure with a definition and a color that were very compact, rather than letting the figure dissolve among the divided brushstrokes of the landscape. The girl in this painting is Aline Charigot, who was to become his wife.*

XVI - Venice, Mist - Washington, Mr. and Mrs. David Lloyd Kreeger - *In the fall of 1881, Renoir visited Italy. He was particularly struck by the warm tones of the Venetian sunsets that inspired several of his paintings. With short, divided brushstrokes he painted San Marco, the lagoon, gondoliers, churches, and palaces immersed in a golden atmosphere.*

XVII - Path in the Forest - New York, private collection - *The clearly separated brushstrokes and the juxtaposition of the spots of color are representative of the impressionist technique which, in order to record the visual sensation of a specific moment, ignores the visual reality of the object and dissolves the contours in a modulation of light and shade. This painting of 1874 is in every sense an "impression."*

XVIII - Madame Monet Reclining on a Sofa - Oeiras, Fundaçao Calouste Gulbenkian - *Renoir's ability to portray an ambience and a figure in a few rapid brushstrokes can be seen in this painting, c. 1873, of Camille Doncieux, the model and wife of Monet since 1865, while she is reading the newspaper "Le Figaro."*

XIX - The Box at the Opera - London, the Courtauld Institute Galleries - *This painting is among Renoir's most famous works. It was shown at the first impressionist exhibition in the studio of the photographer Nadar in 1874, in the same year that the painting was made. Renoir celebrates the beauty of the woman's face, heightened by the light, that becomes the central focus of the painting.*

XX - Portrait of Madame Chocquet in White - Stuttgart, Staatsgalerie - *In March 1875, at the first large public auction organized by the impressionists at the Hotel Drouot, Renoir met Victor Chocquet, a modest and unknown art collector who had a great deal of sensitivity and intuition, and who was able to immediately appreciate the new style of painting. Renoir made several portraits of the Chocquet family.*

XXI - Portrait of Alfred Sisley - Chicago, Courtesy of the Art Institute, Mr. and Mrs. Lewis L. Coburn Memorial Collection - *When Renoir enrolled at the open Academy of the painter Charles Gleyre in 1862 he met Alfred Sisley, with whom he was to maintain a very close friendship. They both had a great love for that art that was to lay the groundwork for the rebirth of French painting.*

XXII - Georgette Charpentier Seated - New York, private collection - *This portrait is of 1876, a period when Renoir became the esteemed friend of the editor Georges Charpentier. He was often a guest of the Charpentier house. The grace and freshness which Renoir expresses in the portraits of the children of the editor, indicate to what extent he was open to the innocent world of children.*

XXIII - Entrance into Society - London, Tate Gallery - *In this painting of 1876, Renoir wants to represent a typical moment of contemporary life: the crowded atmosphere of theater from which a very young woman stands out. In separating the different planes of the composition Renoir delicately brought out the features of the young girl, whereas the figures in the background are only sketched out.*

XXIV-XXV - The Moulin de la Galette - Paris, Musée du Louvre - *Renoir's inclination to depict the life of the times, in its most common and day-by-day aspects, is successfully represented in this painting. In the garden flooded with sunlight the care-free Parisian life is evoked. This work, one of his first large paintings done in 1876, was well received by the public.*

XXVI - Portrait of Madame Alphonse Daudet - Paris, Musée du Louvre - *Frequenting the drawing-room of Madame Charpentier, one of the most important in Paris of the epoch, Renoir met many of the most important exponents of the cultural life of the city, and he often assumed the role of the official social portrait painter, a role which he did not reject, since from these contacts emerged a vivid exchange of ideas.*

XXVII - The Swing - Paris, Musée du Louvre - *This painting was made during the same period as the Moulin de la Galette in 1876. Both have the same luminous atmosphere that is filtered by the branches of the trees, and both resolve in a play of spots of light and shade. The garden depicted in this painting was that of the house on Rue Cortot where he lived at the time.*

XXVIII - Self-Portrait - Cambridge, Mass., Fogg Art Museum, Harvard University, Bequest of Maurice Wertheim - *The delicate plasticity with which Renoir always portrays his models is also evident in this self-portrait of 1876, in which the face is the most detailed area, while the rest of the figure, as well as the background remain relatively undefined.*

XXIX - Algerian Woman - New York, Solomon R. Guggenheim Foundation, the Thannhauser Collection - *In 1881, Renoir had gone to Algeria with his painter friend Corday in order to explore the country that had inspired Delacroix. He painted many landscapes and several portraits of Algerian women, such as this one, with a simple and discreet charm.*

XXX - Madame Charpentier with Her Children - New York, The Metropolitan Museum of Art, The Wolfe Fund - *This large and important canvas, painted by Renoir in 1878, was a key work of his career, for it was exhibited at the Salon in the following year where it was unanimously acclaimed by the critics for the grace and freshness with which the persons and the ambience were depicted.*

13

XXXI - Portrait of Madame Henriot - Washington, National Gallery of Art, Adelaide R. Levy Fund, Inc. Donation - *It was in portraiture that Renoir attained some of his most important results, such as in this stupendous painting of 1877 in which, sacrificing the precision of the drawing for lighter half-tones, he brings out the maximum intensity of the light to the point of evoking a dream-like atmosphere.*

XXXII - Luncheon of the Boating Party - Washington, the Phillips Collection - *In this large painting, begun in 1880 and finished in 1881, Renoir celebrated his world. In a restaurant on the banks of the Seine, on a sunny summer's day, he portrayed his friends, capturing their daily habits, and depicting each of them with a Renaissance-like richness of effects.*

XXXIII - Boatmen at Chatou - Washington, National Gallery of Art - *Having perfectly mastered the impressionistic technique Renoir, in this painting of 1879, depicted one of his favorite spots along the Seine. With short and rapid brushstrokes he brings out the reflection of the light on the water and the luminosity of nature, intermixing within the same atmosphere both the landscape and the people.*

XXXIV - Small Blue Nude - Buffalo, The Albright-Knox Art Gallery - *Renoir felt that the female nude was the best subject to be represented in art, because, as he wrote, "our fantasy cannot imagine anything more beautiful." In this painting of 1879, he exalted the grace of the figure by softening the contours and the background with warmer tones.*

XXXV - The Blond Bather - Turin, private collection - *During his trip to Italy in 1881, Renoir was able to admire Raphael's paintings in Rome and the Roman frescoes at Pompeii. They had an enormous influence on him, as can be seen in the rigorous plastic construction of this painting that he made during his stay in Naples.*

XXXVI - Dance in the Country - Paris, Durand-Ruel Collection - *At the end of 1882, the art dealer Paul Durand-Ruel, a close friend of Renoir's, commissioned him to paint three panels of the same size having as their theme the dance. Renoir used as his models his future wife, Aline Charigot, and his friend, the painter Paul Lhote.*

XXXVII - Dance in the City - Paris, Durand-Ruel Collection - *In this second panel of the dance, as in the first, the female figure predominates in that her personality is clearly represented and accentuated, while the male figure is anonymous. Renoir emphasized the delicate profile of the girl and the luminosity of her dress.*

XXXVIII - The Fish Vendor - Washington, National Gallery of Art - *This female figure, drenched in sunlight, whose contours are caressingly painted by Renoir, fuses in perfect harmony with the landscape. The colors blend completely, enveloping her in warm golden tonalities.*

XXXIX - Sketch for The Bathers - Paris, Paul Pétridès Collection - *This is one of the numerous studies, among which there are two in oil, that were made between 1883 and 1886, as preparatory works for the large canvas of several bathers that Renoir had wanted to paint since 1882, upon his return from his trip to Italy.*

XL-XLI - The Bathers - Philadelphia, the Philadelphia Museum of Art, Mr. and Mrs. Carroll S. Tyson Collection - *This important work, which the artist waited more than three years, to 1887, to paint, testifies to Renoir's matured interests after the great decade of the impressionist movement. He is interested in a new approach to the composition.*

XLII - Maternity - London, private collection - *In this sketch, done in red pencil with white gesso highlighting, one can note Renoir's reaction to the deep crisis when the impressionist techniques were no longer an adequate means of expressing his esthetic ideas. The forms and the drawing of this sketch are executed in an almost forced manner.*

XLIII - Maternity, or a Woman Feeding her Child - New York, private collection - *In this painting of 1886, in which Renoir used as a model his young wife and his first son, the reaction against the danger of dissolving the form in the impressionist manner leads to the strident contrast between the figure, with its precise and clear-cut contour, and the landscape, which has remained a typically impressionistic one.*

XLIV - Child with a Bundle of Grass - San Paolo, Museu de Arte - *Renoir's love for the simplicity of daily life led him, even in the difficult search for a way to overcome the limits of impressionism, to portray rural scenes in which he was able to express himself with great success. In this painting of 1888, the forms are underlined by the luminous touches of the brushwork.*

XLV - The Daughters of Catulle Mendès - London, The Hon. and Mrs. Walter H. Annenberg - *This large canvas, painted in 1888, is considered to be one of Renoir's masterpieces. One can see how he had overcome the crisis of the previous years, developing a technique that permitted him to maintain the impressionistic inspiration of the work, without losing the necessary vigor of the form and drawing.*

XLVI - Vase with Chrysanthemums - Rouen, Musée des Beaux-Arts - *Renoir had always liked to paint flowers and he often included them in his most difficult compositions as a note of color. But he also made many canvases in which flowers were the main subject, as in this painting in which he expresses the harmony of their colors, as well as the vivacity of the movements of the petals.*

XLVII - The Apple Vendor - Cleveland, the Cleveland Museum of Art, Leonard C. Hanna, Jr. Collection - *Renoir did several versions of this painting made during the summer of 1890. Within the delicate impressionist atmosphere Renoir portrayed his young wife with their first-born son, Pierre, and their nephew Edmond seated on the grass.*

XLVIII - Woman Playing the Guitar - Lyons, Musée des Beaux-Arts - *Painted during the last years of the 19th century, this work reveals the result of research into forms and structures with which Renoir was involved in the preceding years. His brushwork now is more fluid and flowing, but it has acquired a textural density that was missing during the impressionist period.*

XLIX - On a Field, or the gathering of flowers - New York, The Metropolitan Museum of Art - *With this painting, done in 1890, Renoir has developed an absolutely original style which allows him to return to the concepts of impressionism while still elaborating a very personal technique. The brushwork is very luminous and the figures stand out of the surrounding landscape.*

L - Girls on the Seashore - Fribourg, Collection of Baron Louis de Chollet - *Having overcome a certain hardness in expressing the lines of the figures during his period of crisis, in this 1894 painting Renoir has again found the luminosity of tones that blend harmoniously with every element of the composition, without losing anything in the precision of the forms. The continuous brushwork renders a plasticity to the entire work.*

LI - Bather Seated on a Rock - Paris, private collection - *This was to be one of Renoir's preferred themes of which he would paint many versions. In this painting of 1892, the artist's exploration of the theme is still evolving, but one can already see that the luminosity of the atmosphere perfectly integrates the figure and its surroundings, delicately shading the contours.*

LII - At the Piano - Paris, Collection of Madame Jean Walter - *In these last years of the 19th century, Renoir often painted a series of works, with one or two people, that are a variation on the same theme, and that express the research that he undertook during those years on the nude and portraits. In this painting of 1892, with its lack of details, one can still detect the use of the impressionistic technique.*

LIII - At the Piano - Paris, private collection - *This version of the theme that he had repeated several times during the same year is probably the last one. The minute description of the interior, of the clothes and faces, does not distract the viewer due to the soft iridescent light that envelops the entire composition and emphasizes the sweetness and the serenity of the moment.*

LIV - Flowers in a Vase - Ireland, private collection - *During the last years of his life Renoir painted many compositions of flowers. They served to deepen his study on color and on their tonal modulations. Roses, as in this painting of the beginning of the century, had a particular interest for him, for they related in their tonalities to the shadings of the body.*

LV - Still Life with Cup and Sugar-bowl - Paris, private collection - *Few artists loved the simple things of everyday life as much as Renoir did. The numerous compositions of household objects are a testimony of this love and expressions of the warmth within him.*

LVI - Houses at Cagnes - Paris, private collection - *During his stay at Cagnes where he lived until his death, Renoir often painted the surrounding landscape, the houses, the plants that attracted him for the luminosity of their hues. In this study of 1905, he depicted with warm and brilliant tones the intense colors of southern France.*

LVII - Le Cros-de-Cagnes - Lausanne, private collection - *In the last period of Renoir's artistic production he intensified the colors of the landscapes, at times with hues that are predominantly red, at other times, such as in this painting of 1905, with bold juxtapositions of greens and blues that mix harmoniously within the work.*

LVIII - Claude Renoir Playing - Paris, Collection of Madame Jean Walter - *The family atmosphere had always inspired Renoir's works. The favorite model of the last years was his third son, whom everyone called Coco. Renoir depicted him during the most spontaneous moments, observing with love the first happy discoveries and experiences of the boy.*

LIX - Self-Portrait with a White Hat - Paris, Durand-Ruel Collection - *The sweetness and the serenity that one feels in this last self-portrait of 1910 that is free of details, faithfully reflects Renoir's happy and candid attitude toward life. His vision of life had permitted him to express the joyous harmony of nature in all of his works.*

LX - Washerwomen at Cagnes - Paris, private collection - *The last period of Renoir's life is the richest, the most immediate, the most mature. Renoir still painted many works with female nudes (the only real stars of his art), such as in this canvas of 1912, with a sureness of the composition, a force in the image, and an intensity of colors that were never superseded.*

LXI - Seated Bather - Chicago, Art Institute - *This is one of the most important works of the last period. It is characterized by the monumentality and breath of the composition and by the conception of the figure, which occupies almost the entire space of the painting. With the boldness of the form of the figure there is an expansion of the color that modulates within infinite shadings of the same tonality.*

LXII - Madeleine Bruno, or the Two Bathers - Paris, private collection - *In painting this canvas in 1916, Renoir, at the height of his artistic maturity, rediscovers the ample forms and the harmony of the balanced gestures of the statues of antiquity. The perfect fusion of the figure with the surroundings creates a pantheistic synthesis of which Renoir had always dreamed.*

LXIII - Walk on the Seashore - Milan, Civica Galleria d'Arte Moderna, Grassi Collection - *The passionate exaltation that Renoir must have felt toward every landscape that inspired him is synthesized in the poetic image of this painting where the figures and the surroundings blend one into the other, giving the work a sense of classical serenity.*

15

II

IV

A. Renoir. 67.

V

VIII

XII

XVIII

XX

XXI

XXIX

XXXIV

XXXVIII

XXXIX

XLII

XLIII

XLVI

XLVIII

L

LVI

LVII

LIX

LXIII

Illustrations from the Picture Archives of Fabbri Editori, Milan
Printed in June 1978, at the graphic plant of Fabbri Editori - Milan, Italy